how2become

KENT TEST BOOKLET

(ENGLISH)

THE
REVISION
SERIES

www.How2Become.com

As part of this product you have also received FREE access to online tests that will help you to pass the Kent Test (English).

To gain access, simply go to:

www.PsychometricTestsOnline.co.uk

Get more products for passing any test or interview at:

www.how2become.com

Orders: Please contact How2become Ltd, Suite 2, 50 Churchill Square Business Centre, Kings Hill, Kent ME19 4YU.

You can order through Amazon.co.uk under ISBN 978-1-910602-38-6, via the website www.How2Become.com or through Gardners.com.

ISBN: 978-1-910602-38-6

First published in 2015 by How2become Ltd.

Typeset for How2become Ltd by Anton Pshinka.

Printed in Great Britain for How2become Ltd by:
CMP (uk) Limited, Poole, Dorset.

Disclaimer

Every effort has been made to ensure that the information contained within this guide is accurate at the time of publication. How2become Ltd are not responsible for anyone failing any part of any selection process as a result of the information contained within this guide. How2become Ltd and their authors cannot accept any responsibility for any errors or omissions within this guide, however caused. No responsibility for loss or damage occasioned by any person acting, or refraining from action, as a result of the material in this publication can be accepted by How2become Ltd.

The information within this guide does not represent the views of any third party service or organisation.

CONTENTS

THE
REVISION
SERIES

INTRODUCTION TO YOUR GUIDE

Welcome to your new booklet, *the 11+ Kent Test, English*. This booklet has been specifically designed to aid anyone who wishes to improve their performance during the English section of the Kent Test.

This booklet primarily focuses on the English section of the Kent Test. We have created other testing booklets similar to this one, for the other sections of the Kent Test assessment.

If you wish to successfully pass all of the stages of the assessment, and thus improve your overall performance, we highly recommend that you take a look at our other revision booklets for 11+ Maths, Verbal Reasoning and Non-Verbal Reasoning.

We wish you the best of luck in your assessment.

THE
REVISION
SERIES

GENERAL TIPS
FOR ENGLISH

GENERAL TIPS FOR ENGLISH

1. Accuracy is key. You need to remain as accurate as possible to ensure high marks. That is why it is important to fully comprehend each question, and understand what the question is actually asking you.

2. Make sure that you undergo practice questions under timed conditions. This will allow you to practice under similar conditions to that of the real test.

3. Practice as many different types of English questions as you can. We have provided you with several different question *types*, in order to enhance your performance. **Please note**, the question types within this guide are merely an indication of the common types of questions that you are likely to encounter during the 11+ assessment.

4. Practice a variety of difficulty levels. If you are finding the practice questions relatively easy, why not practice more difficult questions? This will help to boost your confidence and enhance your skills. If you practice at a variety of difficulty levels, you will be ready to tackle any type of English-related question in the assessment.

5. Make sure that you read through the passages thoroughly. Read through the whole passage once, and then refer back to the passage when it comes to answering the questions. You need to have a good understanding of what the passage is talking about, before attempting the questions.

6. Do not rely upon memory. Once you read the question, go back through the passage – don't rely on your initial reading of the passage. You will have some indication of where the answer is referred to in the passage, so go back through and read that section again.

7. Make sure that you revise literary techniques such as similes, metaphors, personification, alliteration, etc. Having a strong understanding of literary techniques will help you to perform to a higher standard.

8. Questions that ask you to complete the sentence by finding the missing word are best practiced by reading the sentence aloud. That way you will be able to hear whether the sentence reads coherently, with the selected word you have chosen.

9. Brush up on your vocabulary. These types of tests are designed to assess your English and vocabulary skills. Therefore you need to be able to demonstrate a strong level of ability regarding words, phrases and meanings.

10. Make sure that you learn the difference between *past, present* and *future* tenses. You will likely be given questions based on these three areas, and thus it will help if you know the difference between each of the terms.

11. If you want to better your English Comprehension, we also recommend that you spend some time practising questions relating to Verbal Ability. This will allow you to engage with words, sentences and comprehension, which ultimately test the same skills required in the English assessment.

12. Check out our free online psychometric testing and sample questions to make sure that you are fully prepared for your English assessment.

www.PsychometricTestsOnline.co.uk

THE
REVISION
SERIES

EXAMPLE QUESTIONS FOR ENGLISH

READING COMPREHENSION

The large majority of the assessment will focus on your ability to read a passage, and then answer questions relating to that passage.

The key to this type of question, is to make sure that you have read through the passage carefully. The passage is usually numbered (i.e. line numbers are often provided), so that it is easier to locate what the question is referring to.

Types of questions

The types of questions that you will be asked in relation to the passage will vary, but will generally consist of the following:

- Similes;
- Metaphors;
- Alliteration;
- Word Definitions;
- Prefixes and Suffixes;
- Synonyms and Antonyms;
- Homophones;
- Spelling, Grammar and Punctuation.

Within this booklet, we have done our utmost to provide you with an array of different English questions, in order to improve your skills and knowledge regarding English Comprehension.

Please note, the questions in this booklet are NOT THE SAME as the questions in your 11+. Instead, they have been carefully designed to assess similar skills to those that will be assessed during the 11+ assessment.

Make sure that you brush up on the bullet points as listed above. The majority of these questions will appear in some format during your English assessment. Therefore, it is vitally important that you fully grasp the concept of each question type, in order to maximise your overall chances of success.

LITERARY TECHNIQUES

Allegory – stories in which the characters represent abstract ideas or qualities.

Alliteration – repetition of first consonant sounds i.e. 'beautiful, baby boy'.

Hyperbole – a wild exaggeration i.e. 'I am so hungry, I could eat a horse'.

Iambic pentameter – ten-syllable lines of poetry, of which every other syllable is stressed.

Imagery – descriptions of sight, sounds, touch, taste and smell.

Metaphor – A figure of speech that identifies something as being the same as another, unrelated thing. i.e. 'The road was a ribbon of moonlight'.

Satire – work that makes fun of something or someone.

Simile – drawing parallels or comparisons between two things i.e. 'I was cold as an ice cube'.

Onomatopoeia – use of words that sound like what they mean i.e. 'buzz', 'bang'.

Oxymoron – a phrase that is made up of two opposite words i.e. 'bitter sweet'.

Personification – giving an inhuman object, human characteristics.

Pun – the use of a word that plays on multiple meanings.

Irony – language that conveys certain ideas, by saying the opposite.

If you are undertaking an English Comprehension test, you will need to have a strong understanding of literary techniques, and how they are applied within written texts.

We recommend that you practice these literary techniques by coming up with example sentences yourself. So, for each of the above literary techniques, come up with 2-3 sentences, using that literary technique. We have provided space on the next couple of pages for you to write your examples.

Come up with a list of example sentences for the following literary techniques.

Allegory

Alliteration

Hyperbole

Iambic Pentameter

Imagery

Metaphor

Satire

Simile

Onomatopoeia

Oxymoron

Personification

Pun

Irony

We have left you additional space for you to practice any other examples of any other literary device that you wish to practice.

THE
REVISION
SERIES

ENGLISH
(SECTION 1)

Question 1

Complete these words by adding the suffixes *ious* or *ous*.

Ser_____   Mischiev_____   Prec_____   Fur_____

Luxur_____   Outrage_____   Courage_____   Ted_____

Question 2

Underline the correct homophones for the following sentences.

Julie asked for a (peace, piece) of cake.

My mum went to the bank and had to (cue, queue) for an hour.

(Their, There, They're) going to need a bigger boat.

Question 3

Which word does not have a similar meaning to – result?

A	B	C	D
Outcome	Effect	Upshot	Affect

Question 4

Choose a word that relates to both sets of words in the brackets.

(cry, weep)   *(rip, split)*

A	B	C	D
Water	Tear	Cut	Hole

Question 5

Choose a word that relates to both sets of words in the brackets.

(control, manage)   *(frank, honest)*

A	B	C	D
Conduct	Manipulate	Direct	Truthful

Question 6

Write a definition for the following word:

Ludicrous

Question 7

Write a definition for the following word:

Incompetent

Question 8

Write out the following sentence, using the correct spelling and punctuation.

it was a nightmare said kate who was still in shock

Question 9

Write out the following sentence, using the correct spelling and punctuation.

no body no's how difficult it has been these last few years my family have been through soo much and everyday I count my blessings to still have them in my live.

Question 10

Determine whether the following sentences are written in **past**, **present** or **future** tenses.

I will get up on time in the morning.   ------------------

I am eating my dinner.   ------------------

Sammie is going for a run this afternoon.   ------------------

Elliott went swimming.   ------------------

Question 11

Complete the following sentence.

After four hours of looking, the _____ for the _____ puppy was called off.

A – Puppy / lovely

B – Dog / missing

C – Search / missing

D – Party / missing

E – Hunt / search

Answer _____

Question 12

Complete the following sentence.

> *Lucy ---------- her homework and ---------- watched TV.*

A – Finished / decided to

B – Completed / went

C – Started / whilst

D – Finished / then

E – Didn't / instead

Answer [   ]

Question 13

Which of the following sentences has a mistake in its punctuation?

A – Milo was a fluffy, kitten.

B – I have three brothers called Harrison, Ryan and John.

C – My goldfish is yellow, pink and grey.

D – My brother, Joe, is always crying.

E – Although I was nervous, I did it anyway.

Answer [   ]

Question 14

Which of the following sentences has a mistake in its punctuation?

A – Everyone came to my party – except Jason.

B – What is the capital city of Italy?

C – If I could be any animal, I would be an eagle.

D – "Stop it?" shouted the teacher.

E – I drunk a lot of fizzy drink at the party; it made me feel sick.

Answer

Question 15

Which word has the most opposite meaning to – rude?

A – Obscene

B – Crass

C – Inappropriate

D – Gallant

E – Crude

Answer

Question 16

Complete these words by adding the prefixes *mis* or *dis*.

_ _ _ _ _ connect   _ _ _ _ _ lead   _ _ _ _ _ treat   _ _ _ _ _ understood

_ _ _ _ _ honest   _ _ _ _ _ ability   _ _ _ _ _ loyal   _ _ _ _ _ print

Question 17

Choose a word that relates to both sets of words in the brackets.

(rest, interval)   *(damage, smash)*

A	B	C	D
Drop	Wait	Blow	Break

Question 18

Complete the following sentence.

The boy waited _____ for his mother to arrive.

A – Always
B – Patient
C – Patience
D – Patiently
E – Never

Answer [   ]

Question 19

Complete the following sentence.

My friend _____ me to the party.

A – Companied
B – Accompany
C – Accompanied
D – Company
E – Accomplished

Answer [   ]

Question 20

Which word does not have a similar meaning to – atrocious?

A	B	C	D
Barbaric	Ruthless	Cruel	Admirable

Question 21

Which of the following sentences has a mistake in its punctuation?

A – Its not a difficult task.

B – "What do you want for dinner?" asked Jane.

C – If it rains tomorrow, I will not be happy.

D – She was a tall, beautiful girl.

E – My friends Ava, Sophie and Rebecca are staying the night.

Answer

Question 22

Complete the following sentence.

          ---------- *than playing football, Johnny* ---------- *to play tennis instead.*

A – Instead / chose

B – Rather / instead

C – Rather / chose

D – Instead / rather

E – After / chose

Answer

Question 23

Complete the following sentence.

Kevin used the .... to type and the mouse to ....

A – Mouse / type

B – Keyboard / type

C – Mouse / point

D – Typer / mouse

E – Keyboard / point

Answer

Question 24

Write a definition for the following word:

Belittle

_____

_____

_____

ANSWERS TO SECTION 1

Q1. Serious, mischievous, precious, furious, luxurious, outrageous, courageous, tedious.

Q2. (piece), (queue), (They're)

EXPLANATION = Julie asked for a **piece** of cake.

My mum went to the bank and had to **queue** for an hour.

They're going to need a bigger boat.

Q3. D = affect

EXPLANATION = outcome, effect and upshot are all words that have the same meaning as 'result'. Affect has a different meaning to 'result' as it refers to "touching the feelings of something" or "have an emotional impact".

Q4. B = tear

EXPLANATION = tear can be referred to as a 'teardrop', or a 'rip' or 'slit' in something i.e. a tear in trousers.

Q5. C = direct

EXPLANATION = direct can refer to someone who is being 'frank' and 'honest' (taking a direct approach), or it can mean 'control' or 'manage' (to direct something, to take control).

Q6. Your answer should read something like this:

Ludicrous is a term used to describe something that is utterly absurd or foolish.

Q7. Your answer should read something like this:

Someone who is believed to be incompetent can be described as someone who is lacking the correct qualities or skills needed to do something successfully. For example, an incompetent employee is someone who is inadequate at their job.

Q8. "It was a nightmare" said Kate, who was still in shock.

EXPLANATION = the first part of the sentence is being spoken (by Kate), therefore it needs quotation marks. The first letter of the first word needs to be capitalised. 'Kate' is a name, and therefore also needs to be capitalised. A comma is needed after Kate in order for the sentence to flow better. A full stop is needed at the end of the sentence in order to complete the sentence.

Q9. Nobody knows how difficult it has been these last few years. My family have been through so much, and every day I count my blessings to still have them in my life.

EXPLANATION = 'no body' needs to be one word; it also needs a capital letter to begin the sentence. 'No's' is not grammatically correct and instead should be 'knows'. A full stop is needed after the word 'years'. This means that the next word 'my' needs to start with a capital letter. 'Soo' should be 'so'. 'Everyday' needs to be written as 'every day'. 'Live' should be 'life'.

Q10. Future, present, future, past

EXPLANATION = *I will get up on time in the morning* - this is future tense. The situation has not happened yet, and is referring to the next morning i.e. in the future.

I am eating my dinner - if you are doing something, this is present tense i.e. it's happening right now.

Sammie is going for a run this afternoon - if Sammie is going to go, that means she hasn't already, which means this is written in future tense.

Elliott went swimming - if Elliott has already been swimming, this means that the sentence is written in past tense i.e. it's already happened.

Q11. C = search / missing

EXPLANATION = after four hours of looking, the **search** for the **missing** puppy was called off.

Q12. D = finished / then

EXPLANATION = Lucy **finished** her homework and **then** watched TV.

Q13. A = Milo was a fluffy, kitten

EXPLANATION = there should not be a comma after the word 'fluffy'. It doesn't read correctly and is not necessary.

Q14. D = "Stop it?" shouted the teacher.

EXPLANATION = there shouldn't be a question mark after 'stop it'. This is not a question, it is an order, and therefore the words should be followed by an exclamation mark instead.

Q15. D = gallant

EXPLANATION = gallant has the most opposite meaning to rude. Gallant can be defined as someone who shows bravery and chivalry i.e. attentive or heroic.

Q16. Disconnect, mislead, mistreat, misunderstood, dishonest, disability, disloyal, misprint.

Q17. D = break

EXPLANATION = break can mean 'taking a break' i.e. a rest or interval. It can also mean to 'break something' i.e. to 'damage' or 'smash' something.

Q18. D = patiently

EXPLANATION = the boy waited **patiently** for his mother to arrive.

Q19. C = accompanied

EXPLANATION = my friend **accompanied** me to the party.

Q20. D = admirable

EXPLANATION = all of the other words are synonyms of the word atrocious, whereas 'admirable' is the opposite to all of these words.

Q21. A = its not a difficult task

EXPLANATION = 'its' needs to be 'it's' (short for 'it is').

Q22. C = rather / chose

EXPLANATION = **rather** than playing football, Johnny **chose** to play tennis instead.

Q23. E = keyboard / point

EXPLANATION = Kevin used the **keyboard** to type and the mouse to **point**.

Q24. Your answer should read something like this:

The term belittle can be used to describe something which makes it seem less serious. It is a word used to dismiss something or someone as unimportant or put someone down.

THE
REVISION
SERIES

ENGLISH
(SECTION 2)

Question 1

Write a definition for the following word:

Gratitude

Question 2

If the following words were arranged in alphabetical order, which word would come last?

A	B	C	D	E
Petrified	Petroleum	Penalised	Pewter	Perpendicular

Question 3

If the following words were arranged in alphabetical order, which word would come first?

A	B	C	D	E
Astounding	Abysmal	Agitate	Aghast	Apocryphal

Question 4

Which sentence has the correct punctuation?

A – My dog barks all, the time.

B – My mums dad is named steve.

C – "That was unacceptable behaviour" said Kim's teacher.

D – it's there fault.

Answer

Question 5

Complete these words by adding the prefixes *pro* or *pre*.

------ mature   ------ active   ------ logue   ------ dominant

------ serve   ------ spect   ------ long   ------ nounce

Question 6

Determine whether the following sentences are written in **past**, **present** or **future** tenses.

I ran to the park.   ------------------

I am running.   ------------------

I am going to run to the park.   ------------------

Susie had gone for a shower.   ------------------

Question 7

Write a definition for the following word:

Infiltrate

Question 8

Choose a word that relates to both sets of words in the brackets.

(flower, pink)   *(climb, ascend)*

A	B	C	D
Soar	Lift	Rose	Lily

Question 9

Write a definition for the following word:

Ruthless

- -

- -

- -

Barry and Bill work at their local supermarket in the town of Whiteham. Barry works every day except Wednesdays. The supermarket is run by Barry's brother Elliot, who is married to Sarah.

Sarah and Elliot have 2 children called Marcus and Michelle, who are both 7 years old, and they live in the road adjacent to the supermarket. Barry lives in a town called Redford, which is 7 miles from Whiteham.

Bill's girlfriend Maria, works in a factory in her hometown of Brownhaven. The town of Redford is 4 miles from Whiteham and 6 miles from the seaside town of Tenford. Sarah and Elliot take their children on holiday to Tenford twice a year, and Bill usually gives them a lift in his car.

Barry's mum lives in Tenford and he tries to visit her once a week, at 2pm, when he is not working.

Question 10

Which town does Elliot live in?

A – Redford
B – Whiteham
C – Brownhaven
D – Tenford

Answer

Question 11

Using the above passage, Bill and Maria live together in Brownhaven?

A – True
B – False
C – Impossible to say

Answer

Flight A outbound leaves at 8am and arrives at 1pm. The cost of the flight is £69, but this does not include a meal or refreshments. The return flight departs at 3am, and arrives at its destination at 8am.

Flight B outbound leaves at 3pm and arrives at 8pm. The cost of the flight is £97, and this includes a meal and refreshments. The return flight departs at 1pm and arrives at its destination at 5pm.

Flight C outbound leaves at 4pm and arrives at 10pm. The cost of the flight is £70, but this does not include a meal or refreshments. The return flight departs at 10am and arrives at its destination at 4pm.

Flight D outbound leaves at midnight and arrives at 3am. The cost of the flight is £105, which does include a meal and refreshments. The return flight departs at 3pm, and arrives at its destination at 6pm.

Flight E outbound leaves at 5am and arrives at 12noon. The cost of the flight is £39 but includes a meal and refreshments. The return flight departs at 5pm and arrives at its destination at midnight.

Question 12

You want a flight where the outbound flight arrives before 2pm on the day of departure. You don't want to pay any more than £50.

A – Flight A

B – Flight B

C – Flight C

D – Flight D

E – Flight E

Answer

Question 13

You want a return flight that departs in the afternoon between 12noon and 6pm. The cost of the flight must be below £100 and you want a meal. The return flight must arrive at your destination before 6pm

A – Flight A

B – Flight B

C – Flight C

D – Flight D

E – Flight E

Answer

Question 14

You don't want to pay any more than £100 for the flight. You want a meal and the outbound departure time must be in the afternoon.

A – Flight A

B – Flight B

C – Flight C

D – Flight D

E – Flight E

Answer

Janet and Steve have been married for 27 years. They have a daughter called Jessica, who is 25 years old. They all want to go on holiday together but cannot make up their minds as to where to go.

Janet's first choice would be somewhere hot and sunny abroad. Her second choice would be somewhere in their home country, that involves a sporting activity. She does not like hill climbing or walking holidays, but her third choice would be a skiing holiday.

Steve's first choice would be a walking holiday in the hills, somewhere in their home country. His second choice would be a sunny holiday abroad. He does not enjoy skiing.

Jessica's first choice would be a skiing holiday and her second choice would be a sunny holiday abroad. Jessica's third choice would be a walking holiday in the hills of their home country.

Question 15

Which holiday are all the family most likely to go on together?

A – Skiing

B – Walking

C – Sunny holiday abroad

D – Sporting activity holiday

E – Cannot tell

Answer [   ]

Question 16

If Steve and Jessica were to go on holiday together, where would they be most likely to go?

A – Skiing

B – Walking

C – Sunny holiday abroad

D – Sporting activity holiday

E – Cannot tell

Answer

Flat A is located in a town. It is 9 miles from the nearest train station. It has 2 bedrooms and is located on the ground floor. The monthly rental is £450 and the council tax is £50 per month. The lease is for 6 months.

Flat B is located in the city centre and is 2 miles from the nearest train station. It is located on the 3rd floor. The monthly rental is £600 and the council tax is £130 per month. The lease is for 6 months and it has 3 bedrooms.

Flat C is located in the city centre and is 3 miles from the nearest train station. It is located on the 1st floor and has 1 bedroom. The monthly rental is £550 and the council tax is £100 per month. The lease is for 12 months.

Flat D is located in a town. The monthly rental is £395 per month and the council tax is £100 per month. It is located on the ground floor and the lease is for 6 months. It is 18 miles from the nearest train station. The flat has 2 bedrooms.

Flat E is located in a village and is 12 miles from the nearest train station. It has 3 bedrooms and is located on the 2nd floor. The monthly rental is £375 and the council tax is £62 per month. It has a lease for 12 months.

Question 17

You want a flat that is within 10 miles of the nearest train station and is located on the 1st floor or lower. The combined monthly rent/council tax bill must be no greater than £600.

A – Flat A

B – Flat B

C – Flat C

D – Flat D

E – Flat E

Answer

Question 18

You want a flat that has at least 2 bedrooms and has a combined monthly rent/council tax bill which does not exceed £450.

A – Flat A

B – Flat B

C – Flat C

D – Flat D

E – Flat E

Answer

Question 19

You want a flat that has a combined monthly rent/council tax bill that is not in excess of £600, is within 20 miles of the nearest train station and has a lease of 6 months.

A – Flat A or D

B – Flat C

C – Flat B or D

D – Flat E

E – Flat A or E

Answer

Question 20

Complete the following sentence.

Raj ---------- *to go out for dinner* ---------- *he hates cooking.*

A – Wanted / instead

B – Hoped / for

C – Chose / though

D – Instead / because

E – Wanted / because

Answer

Question 21

Which word has the most opposite meaning to – ludicrous?

A – Ridiculous

B – Absurd

C – Foolish

D – Preposterous

E – Superstitious

Answer

Question 22

Write a definition for the following word:

Irrational

Question 23

Complete these words by adding the suffixes **ite** or **ight**.

Appet_ _ _ _ _   Compos_ _ _ _ _ _   Overs_ _ _ _ _ _   Handwr_ _ _ _ _ _

Del_ _ _ _ _ _   Exquis_ _ _ _ _ _   Twil_ _ _ _ _ _   We_ _ _ _ _ _

Question 24

Underline the correct homophones for the following sentences.

After school, she wanted to (prey, pray) at her local church.

It was all (two, to, too) much for her.

On their wild adventures, they ran into a (bear, bare).

ANSWERS TO SECTION 2

Q1. Your answer should read something like this:

Gratitude is the quality of being thankful, showing gratitude or appreciation for something or someone. The term gratitude is a way of showing acknowledgement and recognition.

Q2. D = pewter

EXPLANATION = 'pewter' would be the word that comes last. If the words were arranged in alphabetical order, they would read as follows: *penalised, perpendicular, petrified, petroleum* and *pewter.*

Q3. B = abysmal

EXPLANATION = 'abysmal' would be the first word, if the words were arranged in alphabetical order. They would read: *abysmal, aghast, agitate, apocryphal* and *astounding.*

Q4. C = "That was unacceptable behaviour" said Kim's teacher.

EXPLANATION = the first part of the sentence is being said, so therefore it needs speech marks. The first letter of the first word needs be capitalised. The fact that it is Kim's teacher, means that there needs to be an apostrophe in the word 'Kim's'. A full stop is needed to complete the sentence.

Q5. Premature, proactive, prologue, predominant, preserve, prospect, prolong, pronounce.

Q6. Past, present, future, past

EXPLANATION = *I ran to the shop* – this is past tense because it has already happened.

I am running – this is present tense because it is happening now.

I am going to run to the shop – this is future tense because it is going to happen later, so therefore it's not happening now, and it hasn't happened yet.

Susie had gone for a shower – this is past tense because it has already happened.

Q7. Your answer should read something like this:

Infiltrate means 'to enter or gain access to i.e. intrude or penetrate.' It can also mean to permeate or filter through something.

Q8. C = rose

EXPLANATION = rose can mean a 'type' of flower, or the colour pink (rose is French for pink). Or it can mean to 'ascend', 'rise' or 'climb'.

Q9. Your answer should read something like this:

Ruthless is a word used to show someone who has no pity or compassion for others. A ruthless person can be described as being unsympathetic, cold-hearted or stone-hearted.

Q10. B = Whiteham

EXPLANATION = Elliot lives in Whiteham.

Q11. C = impossible to say

EXPLANATION = you cannot tell from the passage whether or not Bill and Maria live together in Brownhaven.

Q12. E = flight E

EXPLANATION = you want a flight where the outbound flight arrives before 2pm, that automatically rules out Flight B and C. You don't want to pay any more than £50, that rules out Flight A and D. Therefore the correct answer is Flight E.

Q13. B = flight B

EXPLANATION = you want a return flight that departs in the afternoon between noon and 6pm, that rules out Flight A and C. The cost of the flight must be below £100, that rules out Flight D. The return flight must arrive at your destination before 6pm, this rules out Flight E. Therefore the correct answer is Flight B.

Q14. B = flight B

EXPLANATION = you don't want to pay any more than a £100 for the flight, that rules out Flight D. You want a meal, that rules out Flight A and C. You want the outbound departure time to be in the afternoon, which rules out Flight E. Therefore the correct answer is Flight B.

Q15. C = sunny holiday abroad

EXPLANATION = if they were all to go on holiday together, they are most likely going to go on a sunny holiday abroad, because all of them mentioned this as one of their choices.

Q16. C = sunny holiday abroad

EXPLANATION = if Steve and Jessica went on holiday, they are most likely going to go on a sunny holiday abroad, because they both mentioned this as one of their choices.

Q17. A = flat A

EXPLANATION = you want a flat within 10 miles from the nearest train station, that rules out Flat D and E. You want a flat located on the first floor or lower, that rules out Flat B. You want a combined monthly rental/council tax to be no more than £600, this rules out Flat C. Therefore the correct answer is Flat A.

Q18. E = Flat E

EXPLANATION = you want a flat that has at least 2 bedrooms, this rules out Flat C. You want a combined monthly rental/council tax to be no more than £450, this rules out Flat A, B and D. Therefore the correct answer is Flat E.

Q19. A = Flat A or D

EXPLANATION = you want a flat that has a combined monthly rental/council tax to be no more than £600, this rules out Flat B and C. You want your flat to have a lease for 6 months, this rules out Flat E. Therefore Flat A or D are possibilities.

Q20. E = Wanted / because

EXPLANATION = Raj **wanted** to go out for dinner **because** he hates cooking.

Q21. E = superstitious

EXPLANATION = superstitious has the most opposite meaning to ludicrous. Ludicrous can be defined as something that is ridiculous or foolish, whereas superstitious is a word used to demonstrate beliefs in something that is illogical or unprovable.

Q22. Your answer should read something like this:

Irrational is a term used to describe someone's behaviour as being illogical or unreasonable. It is a term which illustrates someone who has been affected by loss or unusual mental clarity i.e. incoherent or crazy.

Q23. Appetite, composite, oversight, handwrite, delight, exquisite, twilight, weight

Q24. (pray), (too), (bear)

EXPLANATION = after school, she wanted to **pray** at her local church.

It was all **too** much for her.

On their wild adventures, they ran into a **bear**.

THE
REVISION
SERIES

ENGLISH
(SECTION 3)

Read the following passage, and answer the following questions.

5. Freight trains are primarily used to transport cargo and goods, as opposed to transporting passengers. The railway network in Great Britain has been used to transport goods of various types and in various contingencies since the early 19th century. Whilst goods traffic in the UK is considerably lower than other countries, it continues to be used, and continues to grow.

10. Rail freight has become vital in regards to Britain's economic success. It is argued that using rail freight has contributed over £800 million to the economy. Not only that, but it has also reduced congestion and carbon emissions, therefore making this use of transportation more environmentally friendly.

15. Whether it is transporting raw materials for manufacturing purposes, fuels for electrical generations or consumer goods, businesses in the UK rely on freight trains to transport the cargo in an environmentally friendly and efficient way.

20. The UK have become more reliant on the use of rail freight, which provides a faster, safer, greener and more efficient way of transporting loads of cargo. It has been said that rail freight is expected to grow in demand by 30% in the next decade. This is equivalent to 240 additional freight trains per day.

25. In order to maintain and uphold this level of continual growth and demand for freight trains, train operating companies will work in partnership with the government to move cargo transports off of the road, and improve the quality of life by substantially reducing carbon emissions.

It is a fact that, on average, a gallon of fuel will move a tonne of goods 246 miles on rail, but only 88 miles by road. Also, each freight train that is used, takes 60 HGV lorries off the road, ultimately helping carbon emissions.

30.   The First World War was described as the "Railway War". Thousands of tonnes of supplies and munitions were distributed all over Great Britain, and dispatched from ports in the South East, to France and to the Front Line. A number of programmes were instigated in order for railways to meet the huge demands of the wartime. The Common

35.   User Agreement, conducted under the Coal Transport Act of 1917 are two examples of programmes that ultimately enabled better railway services. Over 100 train operating companies collaborated on these programmes and worked together to aid national interest.

Question 1

What do freight trains carry?

A – Passengers

B – Cargo

C – Passengers and cargo

D – Cannot be determined

Answer

Question 2

How long have freight trains been in use in Great Britain?

A – Early 17th century

B – Late 17th century

C – Early 18th century

D – Late 18th century

E – Early 19th century

Answer

Question 3

The use of rail freight in Britain has been extremely vital in regards to…

A – Government success

B – Train Operating Companies becoming more popular

C – Economic success

D – Transport safety

E – Cannot be determined

Answer

Question 4

On average, how much has rail freight contributed to the economy?

A – £600 million

B – £800 million

C – £300 million

D – £500 million

E – £900 million

Answer

Question 5

Which **two** of the following answers can be concluded from rail freight being more environmentally friendly? Two answers required.

A – Reduces carbon emissions

B – Reduces the use of lorries

C – Reduces cost

D – Reduces waiting times

E – Reduces numerous transportation methods

Answer [   ]

Question 6

On average, a gallon of fuel for freight trains can move a tonne of goods how far?

A – 88 miles

B – 100 miles

C – 246 miles

D – 276 miles

E – 44 miles

Answer [   ]

Question 7

On average, a gallon of fuel for road usage can move a tonne of goods how far?

A – 246 miles

B – 44 miles

C – 102 miles

D – 88 miles

E – 70 miles

Answer [   ]

Question 8

If a freight train is used, how many HGV lorries are taken off the road?

A – 40

B – 60

C – 30

D – 70

E – 80

Answer [   ]

Question 9

How much are freight trains expected to grow in demand within one decade?

A – 20%

B – 70%

C – 50%

D – 40%

E – 30%

Answer

Question 10

If freight trains continue to grow at the rate that is expected, how many additional freight trains will be used per day?

A – 210

B – 240

C – 200

D – 180

E – 190

Answer

Question 11

How many train companies collaborated on the programmes that were instigated during the First World War?

A – Over 50

B – Over 60

C – Over 20

D – Over 80

E – Over 100

Answer

Question 12

What was the name of the Act that enabled better transport services during World War I?

A – Coal Transport Act 1921

B – Coal Transport Act 1917

C – Coal Transport Act 1912

D – Coal Transport Act 1931

E – Coal Transport Act 1940

Answer

Question 13

What was the First World War also known as?

A – Britain's War

B – British Railway War

C – Front Line War

D – Railway War

E – Cannot be determined

Answer

Question 14

Where were the supplies being shipped? **Two** answers required.

A – Germany

B – France

C – Front Line

D – England

E – Cannot be determined

Answer

ANSWERS TO SECTION 3

Q1. B = cargo

Q2. E = early 19th century

Q3. C = economic success

Q4. B = £800 million

Q5. A = reduces carbon emissions, D = reduces congestion

Q6. C = 246 miles

Q7. D = 88 miles

Q8. B = 60

Q9. E = 30%

Q10. B = 240

Q11. E = over 100

Q12. B = Coal Transport Act 1917

Q13. D = Railway War

Q14. B = France, C = Front Line

THE
REVISION
SERIES

ENGLISH
(SECTION 4)

Read the following passage, and answer the following questions.

5.

10.

15.

20.

25.

The railway system of Great Britain is one of the oldest in the world. The first steam locomotive was used in Britain's nation, and has become a paramount feature of contemporary society.

The arrival of railways has contributed to the dramatic growth in industrialisation during the nineteenth century, and has ultimately had profound impacts on social and economic changes. The railway 'filled a void' that other forms of transport could not. Railways were able to provide an efficient, fast, cost effective and environmentally friendly service that catered for the needs of many people.

The history of the railways in Great Britain is remarkable. The incredible changes that have been made over hundreds of years are remarkable, and can only be described as the 'transformation of transport'. In 1804, the first successful steam locomotive ran on wheels, and was used to transport iron across a track of nine miles. Built by Richard Trevithick, the locomotive – 'the Penydarren', was the world's first steam engine to run on rails.

Since the early 19th century, railways have continued to develop and are now a strong infrastructure within hundreds of societies. During the First World War, the Government took over and ran the railways until 1921, when private railway companies regained control. During 1921, an Act was passed in Parliament which submerged four railway companies: known simply as the 'British Rail'.

During 1940 in the Second World War, the companies effectively worked together to help Britain's war efforts, and in the late 1940's, these railways were nationalised and formed 'British Railways', which was implemented under the Transport Act. In the 50's, society saw a modernised change in regards to railway services. Diesel and electrical trains were introduced, and started to replace the steam locomotive trains.

30.   In 1960, the railways were re-organised in order to try and make money. Secondary routes and branch lines closed. As rationalisation took hold, one-third of the pre-1948 networks closed. A giant leap was undertaken in the 70's, and saw the introduction of the 'high-speed diesel-electric' service trains, and by 1990 both main

35.   coastal express routes, the East and West Coast Main Lines, had been electrified between central Scotland and London.

In 1994, the Channel Tunnel opened and began the service from England to France. This exponential growth in regards to the railway services has considerably changed over the years, and will continue

40.   to adapt.

In 2011, the number of journeys in Great Britain between 2010 and 2011 reached a record breaking 1.16 billion. As of 2013, British railways are believed to be the second safest in Europe (after Luxembourg), and ultimately deliver a modernised service for both local

45.   and national railway routes.

Question 1

Where was the first steam locomotive train used?

A – China

B – Germany

C – France

D – Britain

E – Spain

Answer

Question 2

The railway was able to do what, that other transportation methods could not?

A – Create profits

B – Fill a void

C – Reduce carbon emissions

D – Help industrialise society

E – Create transport for the middle classes

Answer

Question 3

In what year was the first running steam locomotive train made?

A – 1800

B – 1901

C – 1821

D – 1804

E – 1904

Answer

Question 4

What was the name of the 'mechanical genius' who built the first steam locomotive train?

Answer

Question 5

What was the first steam locomotive train called?

Answer

Question 6

In 1921, an Act in Parliament was implemented and saw the introduction of...

A – 'British Railways'

B – 'Great British Railways'

C – 'The four rails'

D – 'British Rail'

E – Cannot be determined

Answer

Question 7

What was the name of the Act in 1940 that nationalised the four railways?

A – Transportation Act

B – Local Transport Act

C – Transport Act

D – National Transport Act

E – Cannot be determined

Answer

Question 8

What fraction of the pre-1948 services closed in 1960?

A – One half

B – One quarter

C – One fifth

D – One third

E – Three thirds

Answer

Question 9

What type of trains were introduced in 1970?

A – High speed

B – Diesel

C – Electrical

D – Steam

E – All of the above

Answer

Question 10

What opened in 1994?

A – Medway Tunnel

B – Bradway Tunnel

C – The Channel Tunnel

D – Redhill Tunnel

E – Dartford Tunnel

Answer

Question 11

Between 2010 and 2011, the number of journeys reached a record breaking…

A – 1.61 billion

B – 1.16 billion

C – 1.66 billion

D – 1.16 million

E – 6.16 billion

Answer

Question 12

Where is considered to have the safest railway in Europe?

Answer

Question 13

What service does the Channel Tunnel offer? I.e. England to...?

Answer [   ]

Question 14

In what year did private train companies regain control of the railway services?

A – 1984

B – 1904

C – 1911

D – 1927

E – 1921

Answer [   ]

ANSWERS TO SECTION 4

Q1. D = Britain

Q2. B = fill a void

Q3. D = 1804

Q4. Richard Trevithick

Q5. 'The Penydarren'

Q6. D = British Rail

Q7. C = Transport Act

Q8. D = one third

Q9. A = high speed

Q10. C = the Channel Tunnel

Q11. B = 1.16 billion

Q12. Luxembourg

Q13. France

Q14. E = 1921

THE REVISION SERIES

ENGLISH
(SECTION 5)

Read the following passage, and answer the following questions.

It's been 11 months and 14 days since my carefully constructed world came crashing down into a thousand little pieces. My life was torn to merciless shreds, just like the car that my mother and I were in.

5.　Little did I know how one moment can change your life forever. I thought I had so much time to make memories with the one person that I relied upon most. I have been forlorn and melancholy for almost a year now, and I am struggling to grasp the concept of 'it gets easier with time'. That to me seems unimaginable.

10.　I remember the sharp sounds of the brakes. I remember the moment our car collided with a patch of glistening ice that covered the country roads. I try to recall the impact, but my mind goes blank. It is like a hole in my memory. My life is in 1000 jigsaw pieces, which I cannot piece back together.

15.　I saw nothing, only an expanse of darkness. I woke to the loud voices of people who seemed to be in close proximity, but was unable to touch them. I opened my eyes to see police, paramedics… all hovering around the car, trying to open the doors and assist us.

I reached out my shaking arm towards my mum. I needed to know
20.　if she was okay. I needed to know that she was there. I cried out her name, but I got no response.

I lay frozen in my seat waiting for help. All I can remember is looking up at the dark night sky, with flashes of bright white lights that were shining down on me.

25.　I tried to stay awake, but I kept drifting off.

The next thing I remember was waking up in the hospital. Wires, oxygen masks, machines; all signs of what had happened the night before.

30. A sudden glimmer of hope swept through my body with the recollection that my mum would be by my bedside. And yet the sheer panic I felt after establishing that she wasn't there, is a feeling that I will never forget.

"Mum! Mum! I need you Mum!" cries of desperation, vulnerability and solitude. Something that no 16 year old should ever have to
35. confront. No one was telling me anything, and I had no idea where my mum was or what had happened. I needed answers.

A voice, a calm, soft voice that sounded ever so familiar. A voice that I always responded to and always felt comforted by… Mum! The soft whispers reassuring me that she was there, and that I would be
40. okay, provided me with a few seconds of comfort and relief. Then I realised it was all in my head. I felt heartbroken. I've never experienced the feeling of being heartbroken before, but I knew that I was! And it was from that moment, I knew that my life would never be the same again.

Question 1

Which of the following reasons best describes why the passage is written in first person?

A – The reader wants to put their views across.

B – It's an account of the author's experience.

C – It is an account of events, creating an emotional relationship with its readers.

D – Provide a sense of belonging and reassurance.

Answer [   ]

Question 2

"My life was torn to merciless shreds" (line 2/3). What does the word 'merciless' refer to in this instance?

A – Unstoppable

B – Cruel

C – Inevitable

D – Unfair

Answer [   ]

Question 3

"My life was torn to merciless shreds, just like the car that my mother and I were in" (line 2/3). What literary technique is used in this sentence?

A – Metaphor

B – Paradox

C – Juxtaposition

D – Simile

Answer

Question 4

"I have been forlorn and melancholy for almost a year now" (line 7/8). What does the word 'forlorn' mean?

A – Sad and resentful

B – Hopeless and lonely

C – Lonely and bitter

D – Hopeless and disorientated

Answer

Question 5

"My life is in 1000 jigsaw pieces, which I cannot piece back together" (line 13/14). What literary technique is used in this sentence?

A – Simile

B – Oxymoron

C – Analogy

D – Pathos

Answer

Question 6

The way the author uses the phrase 'it gets easier with time' (line 8/9), implies that they think it is…

A – Impossible

B – Absurd

C – Ironic

D – Dubious

Answer

Question 7

On line 23, the author refers to white bright lights. What is the most plausible explanation for these lights?

A – Oncoming traffic

B – A sign of going blind

C – Being partially conscious

D – The lights from the paramedics and police working on the car

Answer

Question 8

The overall tone of the passage is…

A – Hopeful

B – Pessimistic

C – Downhearted

D – Overwhelmed

Answer

Question 9

What kind of text is the above passage most likely taken from?

A – A fairy tale

B – A children's story

C – A biography

D – A business report

Answer

Question 10

On line 15, which word has the most similar meaning to the word "expanse"?

A – Area

B – View

C – Image

D – Large

Answer

Question 11

On line 35, what does the term "confront" mean?

A – Something that happens

B – Face up to and deal with

C – A way to measure something's unusualness

D – Faced with something unexpectedly

Answer

Question 12

On line 16, what does the term "proximity" mean, in context of the passage?

A – A type of measurement

B – Nearness in time

C – Person's presence

D – Nearness in space

Answer

Question 13

On line 22, the author uses the word "frozen" to indicate what?

A – Their cold body

B – Their mother's immobile body

C – Their motionless body

D – Their mother's cold body

Answer

Question 14

On line 1, the author uses the phrase "my carefully constructed world". What does the word "constructed" mean in this context?

A – Knocked down

B – Biased

C – Built up

D – Safe

Answer

ANSWERS TO SECTION 5

Q1. C = It is an account of events, creating an emotional directness with its readers.

EXPLANATION = first person narration is often used to create an emotional response with its readers, which draws them in to a specific voice or personal situation.

Q2. B = cruel

EXPLANATION = the use of the word 'merciless' demonstrates an act or event that is cruel and ruthless. The fact that the passage is based on a car accident, reinforces how the teenager (who is the narrator of the passage) describes the accident as cruel and unforgiving.

Q3. D = simile

EXPLANATION = "my life torn to merciless shreds, just like the car that my mother and I were in" is a simile. The use of the word 'like' demonstrates that it is a simile, because it compares the similarities of two very different things.

Q4. B = hopeless and lonely

EXPLANATION = the passage clearly illustrates how the teenager is feeling lonely, melancholy and hopeless after the car accident. Therefore the term 'forlorn' is used to reinforce the teenager's emotions.

Q5. C = analogy

EXPLANATION = the author uses a puzzle as an analogue for life, whereby you have certain pieces that make up your life in order to complete it. The author suggests that trying to find the missing pieces can be extremely difficult, just like when you encounter difficult times and need to work through them.

Q6. A = impossible

EXPLANATION = the author states that situations like these 'get easier with time'. Yet, in the context of the passage, the author cannot possibly imagine it getting any easier. It is still a recent event, and therefore believes that this statement is far-fetched.

Q7. D = the lights from the paramedics and police working on the car

EXPLANATION = the most plausible explanation for the bright white lights, in this case, is that the car accident happened when it was getting dark, so the paramedics and police probably had some sort of lighting equipment to be able to do their job in the dark.

Q8. C = downhearted

EXPLANATION = the overall tone of the passage is extremely down-heartened. The author conveys themselves as lonely and melancholy.

Q9. C = a biography

EXPLANATION = the text in the passage is most likely from a biography. Out of all of the other answer options, this makes the best sense.

Q10. A = area

EXPLANATION = the most similar meaning to the word 'expanse' is 'area'. Expanse can be defined as 'a wide continuous area of something'.

Q11. B = face up to and deal with

EXPLANATION = the term 'confront' is something that a person has to 'face up to and deal with'.

Q12. C = person's presence

EXPLANATION = the term 'proximity' can be defined as a 'nearness in space, time or relationship'. In the context of the passage, the word is most likely to refer to the nearness of another person.

Q13. C = their motionless body

EXPLANATION = the term "frozen" is referring to the individual's motionless body i.e. they are unable to move.

Q14. C = built up

EXPLANATION = the term "constructed" in the sentence mostly refers to how their lives had been carefully built up prior to the accident.

THE
REVISION
SERIES

ENGLISH
(SECTION 6)

Read the following passage, and answer the following questions.

Damp, dirty, dreary. Signs of an untouched room. Blue and grey bricks absorbed the cold air that filled the room. The air was as bitter as a bad arctic breeze during a winter's night.

5.   A single glistening light projected from the last dying-out candle. The dim, hazy glow flickered across the walls, moving to an unseen rhythm. The lone window, high on the back wall, was frosted over. Peering out, all I could see was the outcast shapes of the woods about 50 yards from the cabin. A small gleam of moonlight streamed through the window.

10. The ambiance of such a room provided a precarious, dense and dark mood. Something did not sit right. Something did not feel right. The longer I was in this cold, down-beaten and eerie room, the more I felt like someone was watching.

When you sense that someone is watching you; paranoia plays on
15. your mind, like a lion spying on its prey.

As time went by, peculiar things began to prove my instincts correct. The sound of someone else's footsteps and occasional whispers filled my body with fear. As the night progressed, and the moon brightened, I looked across the window in panic. I looked back!
20. Nothing! I swear I just saw.... Maybe I was delirious or maybe it did happen.

I ignored what I saw, and continued to sit in the middle of the empty room. I felt so small. I'm 5 ft 9 inches tall; I've never once felt small. But now, in this large room, I felt smaller than ever before. Like a
25. baby looking up from its cot at the rest of the world.

I rubbed my eyes, and looked up again. There it was! An indication of life, other than myself, here, in this very room. The glistening moon-

30.

light cast a shadow in the window. As my eyes slowly looked up from the floor, I saw two slim and long shadows dangling and sway-ing from underneath the window ledge. They were legs. I looked up and saw a whitish grey silhouette of a girl who could be no more than 6 or 7. She sat there, looking at me. Wearing a silk night gown, she had her hands clenching her neck, smiling.

35.

I stood up in shock. I know what I saw and I'm not deluded. I rubbed my eyes again and looked back to the window, she had gone. Noth-ing in the window except the frosty ice. I turned slightly, and right there, about 30 centimetres away from where I was stood, was the girl, still clasping her neck, still smiling...

Question 1

"Damp, dirty, dreary" (line 1). What literary technique is this?

A – Simile

B – Metaphor

C – Personification

D – Alliteration

Answer

Question 2

If you had to choose from the following titles, which title best fits with the contents of the passage?

A – Happy Families

B – The Bear in the Forest

C – Spooks

D – Everybody loves Jaya

Answer

Question 3

Which of the following terms is NOT mentioned in the passage?

A – Candle

B – Night gown

C – Baby

D – Curtains

Answer

Question 4

Which of the following, taken from the passage, is using the literary technique of a simile?

A – "The more I felt like someone was watching".

B – "The glistening moonlight cast a shadow in the window".

C – "Like a lion spying on its prey".

D – "She had her hands clenching her neck".

Answer

Question 5

Write another sentence, taken from the passage, which illustrates the use of a simile.

Question 6

On line 24/25, the author refers to babies looking up from their cot. Give one reason as to why the author uses this particular writing style in relation to the rest of the passage.

Question 7

On line 10, the author uses the word "precarious". What does this word mean in terms of how it is used in the passage?

A – Illustrating the uncertainties the room possesses.

B – Reinforces that the room is home to someone.

C – Demonstrating the possible implications of the room.

D – Highlights the importance of remaining doubtful.

Answer

Question 8

On line 10, the author uses the word "dense". Which of the following answer options is most similar in meaning?

A – Dark

B – Light

C – Compacted

D – Subtle

Answer

Question 9

On line 10, the author uses the word "ambiance". Which of the following answer options is most similar in meaning, in context of the passage?

A – Climate

B – Atmosphere

C – Conditions

D – Background

Answer

Question 10

On line 34, the author uses the word "deluded". Write a brief definition of this word.

Question 11

On line 15, the author uses the phrase "like a lion spying on its prey". Which of the following bests describes what the author is trying to convey here?

A – To illustrate that the person is being compared to a lion.

B – To demonstrate the battle of conflict between lions and their prey.

C – To illustrate that the person is being compared to prey.

D – To suggest that the person is fierce and in control; like the lion.

Answer

Question 12

Throughout the passage, the author is referring to this idea of being watched. Which of the following emotions best describes how a person would be feeling if they thought they were being watched?

A – Confused

B – Apprehensive

C – Demeaned

D – Unaffected

Answer

Question 13

On line 27, the author uses the word "glistening". Which of the following words is NOT similar in meaning?

A – Shine

B – Sparkle

C – Dismal

D – Flicker

Answer

Question 14

The description of the frosty window in the last paragraph, allows the author to…

A – Demonstrate what time of year it is.

B – Make the ambiance of the surroundings more eerie and isolating.

C – Suggest that there is no way out.

D – Highlight the importance the window plays in the context of the passage.

Answer

ANSWERS TO SECTION 6

Q1. D = alliteration

EXPLANATION = alliteration is a literary technique that comprises words each starting with the same letter.

Q2. C = Spooks

EXPLANATION = 'Spooks' seems like the only reasonable title that you can use in association with the passage. It has ghostly connotations.

Q3. D = curtains

EXPLANATION = nowhere in the passage does it mention anything about 'curtains'. All of the other answer options are briefly mentioned.

Q4. C = "like a lion spying on its prey"

EXPLANATION = 'like a lion spying on its prey' is the only answer option that demonstrates the literary technique of a simile.

Q5. Your answer should read like this:

"Like a baby looking up from its cot at the rest of the world".

Q6. Your answer should read something like this:

The author uses the phrase "like a baby looking up from its cot at the rest of the world" to demonstrate vulnerability. Babies are small, fragile and vulnerable and therefore require looking after. This is similar to the person in the story, who is feeling vulnerable and small. The use of the simile allows the reader to understand how the person is feeling in such circumstances, and comparing them to a baby, reinforces just how fragile, scared and lonely that person is feeling.

Q7. A = illustrating the uncertainties the room possesses.

EXPLANATION = the term 'precarious' is used to demonstrate the dangers that the room may possess.

Q8. C = compacted

EXPLANATION = 'dense' can be defined as something that is 'closely compacted in substance'.

Q9. B = atmosphere

EXPLANATION = 'ambiance' can be defined as 'the character and atmosphere of a place'.

Q10. Your answer should read something like this:

Deluded is a term that can be used to make sense of something that is not actually true. It is a word that can be used to describe something or someone being misled, or deceived through mind or judgement.

Q11. C = to illustrate that the person is being compared to prey

EXPLANATION = within the passage, it is clear that the author uses the phrase "like a lion spying on its prey", to illustrate that the person is the prey, and the unknown 'thing' in the room is the lion.

Q12. B = apprehensive

EXPLANATION = if you were being watched, the most likely emotion that you would be feeling is 'apprehensive'. Knowing that someone might be watching you is enough to put you on edge and make you nervous.

Q13. C = dismal

EXPLANATION = the only word from the answer options listed that does not mean the same as 'glistening' is 'dismal'. Glistening means to shine bright, sparkle or flicker, whereas dismal is a word used to describe something that is dull and gloomy.

Q14. B = make the ambiance of the surroundings more eerie and isolating

EXPLANATION = the description of the frosty window in the last paragraph is used to make the ambiance of the surroundings seem more eerie and isolated. With the setting of the cabin and the woods, the frosty window can be used to reinforce the isolation and coldness that the person is experiencing.

THE
REVISION
SERIES

ANSWERING
YOUR
QUESTIONS

You have now reached the end of your Kent Test booklet for the English assessment. You should now be confident enough to undergo your assessment feeling fully prepared. Before you go, we recommend that you read through our final top tips on how to answer the questions. You can use these tips in practice, and in your assessment.

Remember, for each exam in the Kent Test, you will be provided with a testing booklet and an answer booklet. These will be similar to the following:

- Maths and English Testing Booklet
- Maths and English Answer Sheet
- Reasoning Testing Booklet
- Reasoning Answer Sheet

You need to read the questions in the testing booklet and choose the correct answer, which you <u>MUST</u> then write on the answer sheet provided. When you take the Kent Test, only the answers written on the answer sheet will be marked. Any other written work or rough drafts on paper or in the testing booklet, will not be marked.

Make sure that at the start of your Kent Test, you take the time to read through the set of instructions on the front of your examination booklet. This will tell you everything you need to know regarding the Kent Test, including how to use the answer booklet and where to write your answers.

- Make sure that you mark your chosen answer to the corresponding question number. For example, if you answered question 5, make sure that you mark the answer to question 5!

- Any rough work, drafts or calculations should not be written on the answer sheet. Instead you can ask for extra sheets of paper or write them in your testing booklet. (Any additional paper or the testing booklet will not be marked!)

Example Answer Sheet

Here is a basic example marking sheet which gives you some indication of what you can expect in your assessment. For example, if you chose answer option 'B' as the correct answer for question 1 on the English test, you would mark a line in pencil or pen, horizontally through the box (as shown).

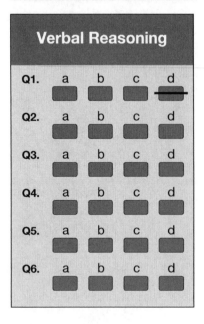

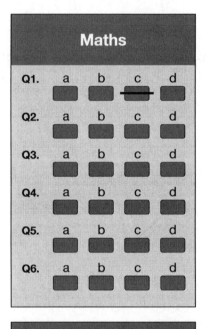

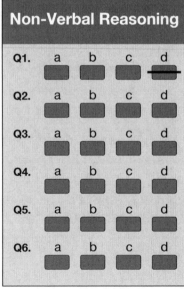

Good luck with your 11+ Kent Test, English. We wish you the very best of luck with all your future endeavours!

The how2become team

The How2become team

how2become

**Get more books, manuals, online tests
and training courses at:**

www.how2become.com